Rätseln mit Spaß

Englisch

Almuth Bartl

Illustriert von Angela Weinhold

arsEdition

Full House

Die Namen der 10 abgebildeten Dinge findest du auch im Haus auf der Nachbarseite. Streiche die Wörter rechts mit Farbstift durch!

chair

radio

sofa

bed

box

table

stove

clock

shelf

armchair

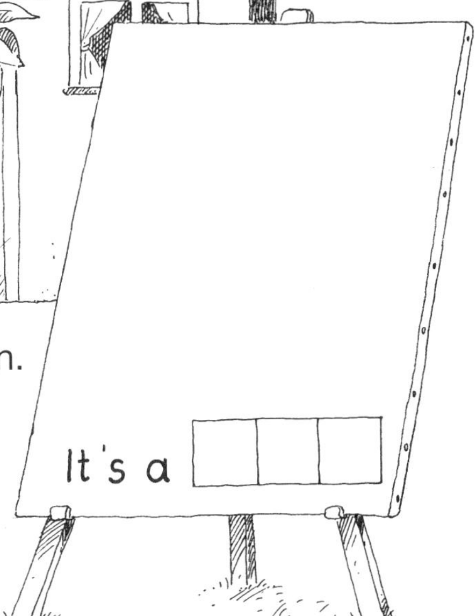

Drei Buchstaben sind übriggeblieben. Sie ergeben zusammengesetzt den Namen eines Tieres, das auch in diesem Haus wohnt. Kannst du es auf die Tafel zeichnen?

Übrigens: Die Lösungen für alle Rätsel findest du im Buch ab Seite 60.

The scrambled crossword Puzzle

Sortiere die Buchstaben, und schreibe die richtigen Wörter in die Kästchen auf der rechten Seite.

1

n a k s e

2

o n i l

3

g i t r e

4

e s e h p

5

h e s r o

6

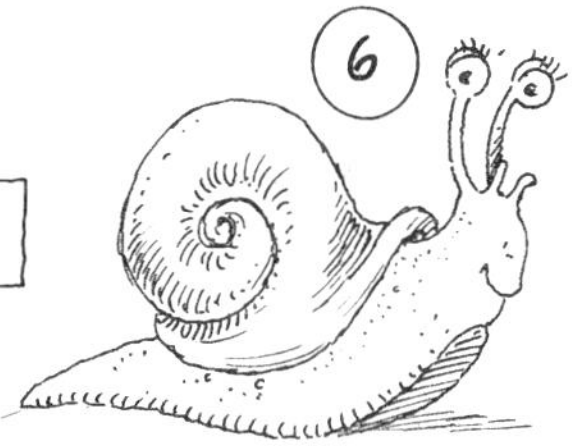

n a l i s

7

n a t

8

t a c

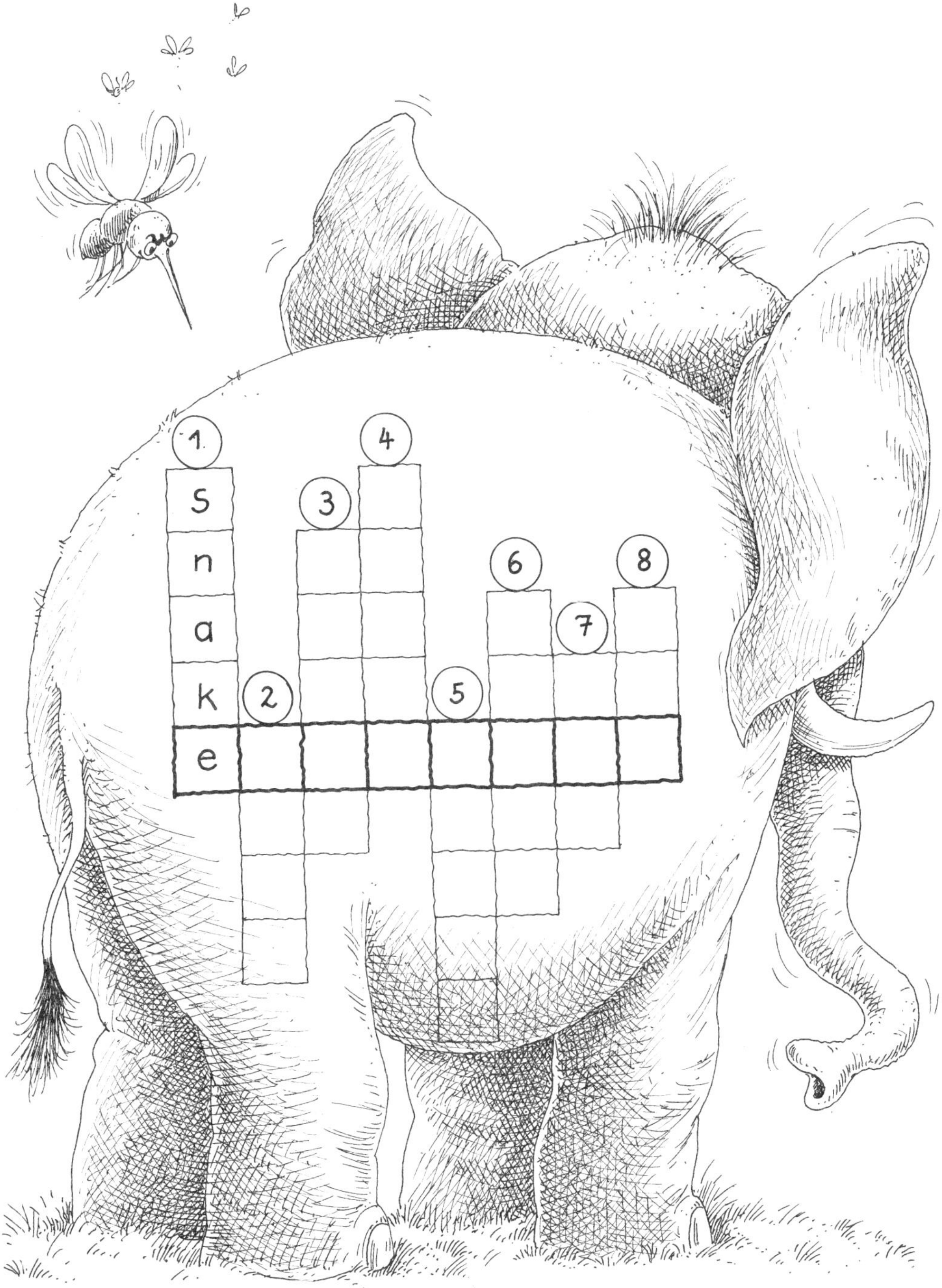
1
2
3
4
5
6
7
8
s
n
a
k
e

12 months in a year

January

February

March

April

May

June

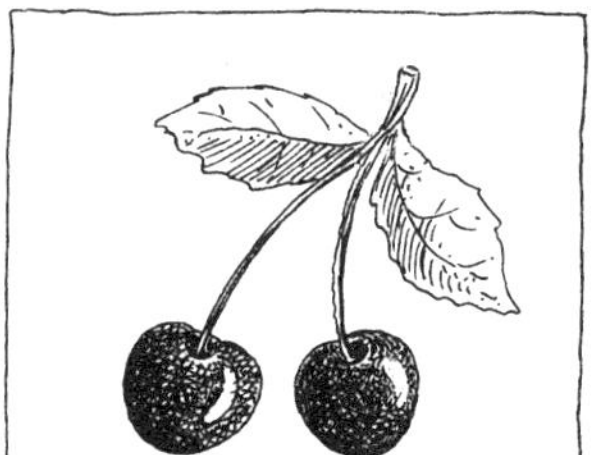
July

August

September

October

November

December

Trage die jeweiligen Monatsnamen in das Rätselgitter ein!
Beispiel: 6th month (6. Monat) = June

12th month

3rd month

7th month

9th month

6th month

2nd month

4th month

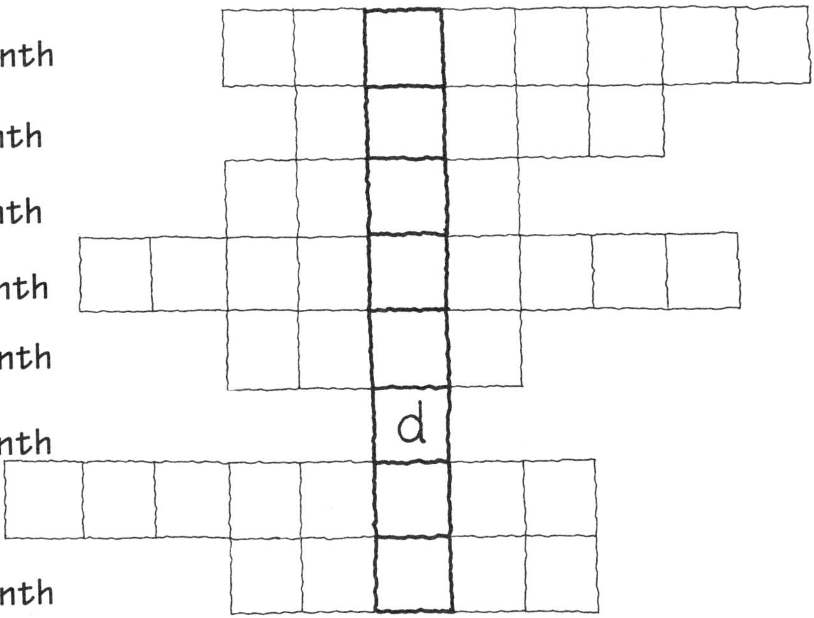

Remember!
The months of the year are proper nouns. They always begin with a capital letter!

Where are the girls going to?

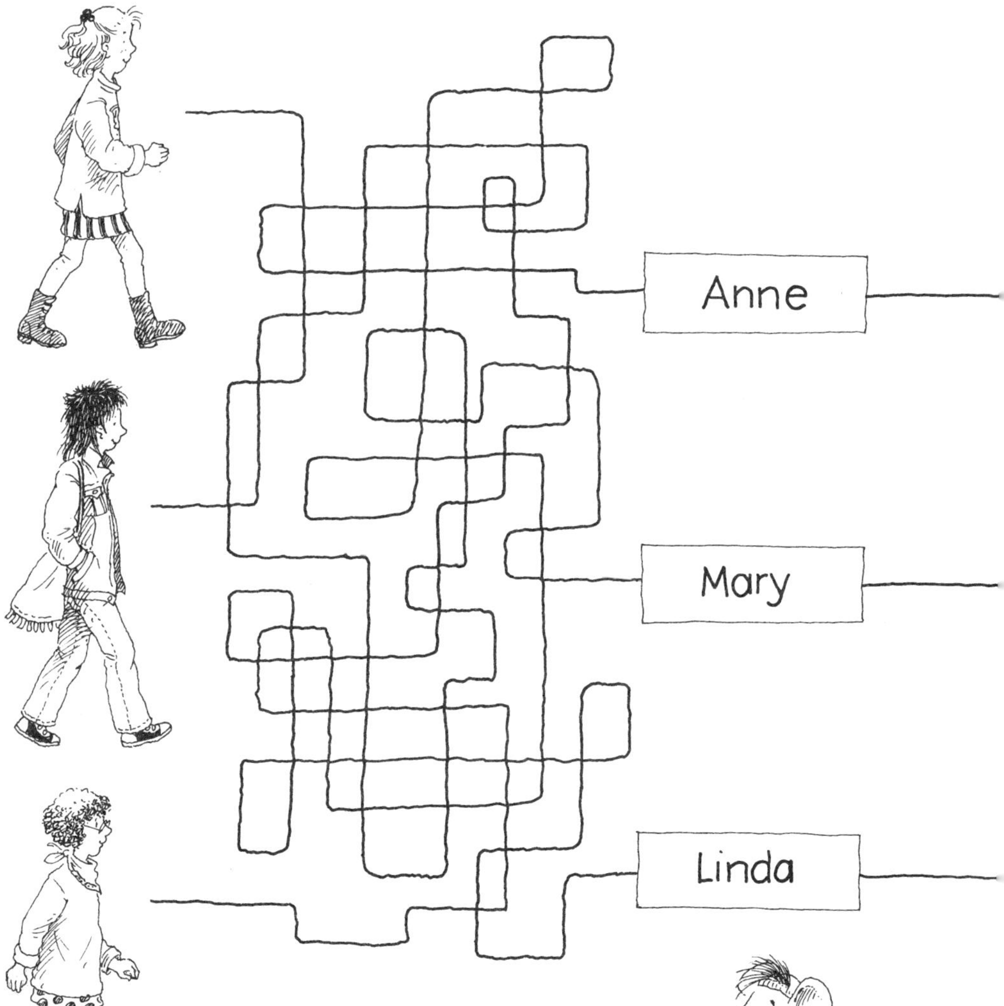

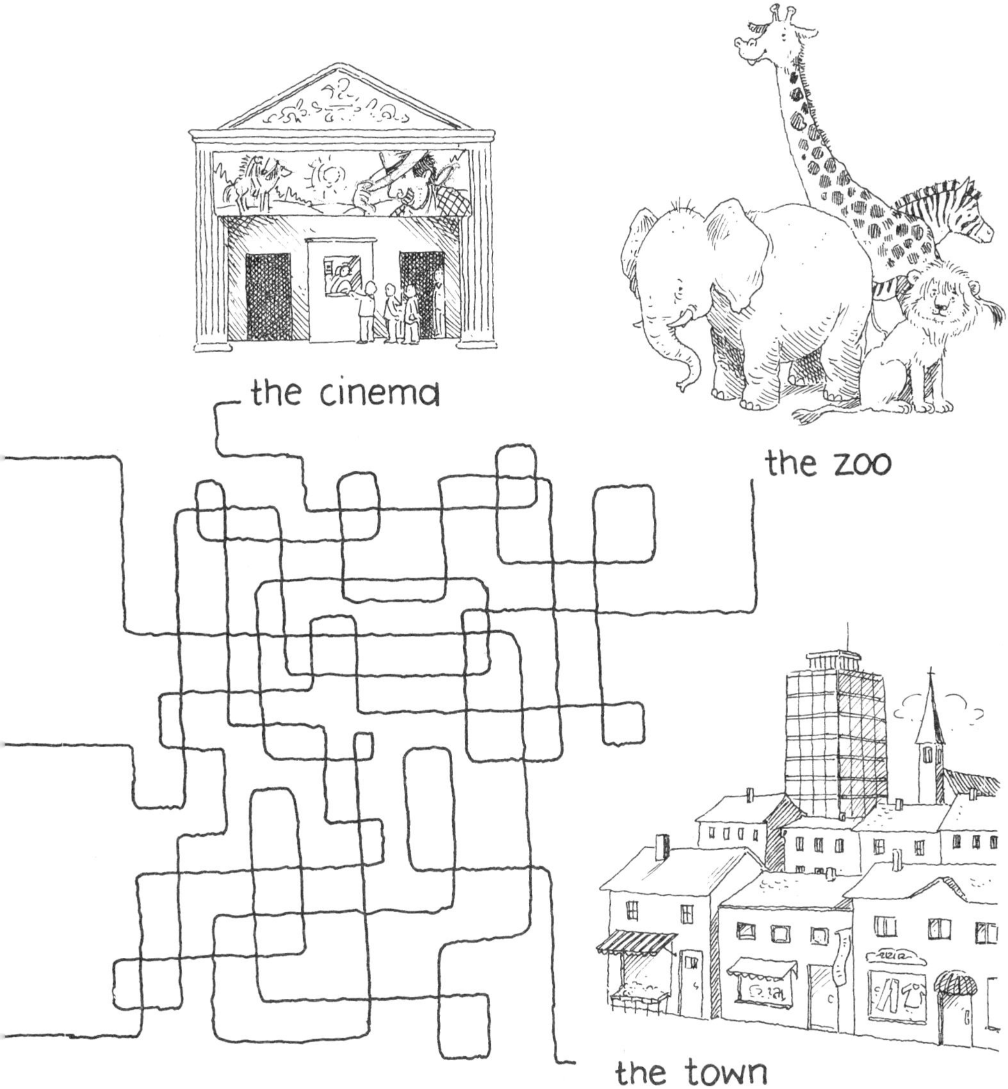

Bilde Sätze!

Anne is going to ______________________________

Mary ______________________________

Linda ______________________________

Clothes

Im Schrank findest du eine Menge Anziehsachen. Aber Vorsicht! Drei Dinge gehören nicht in den Kleiderschrank. Streiche sie durch!

I'm wearing a red pullover with blue stripes, blue trousers, green socks and brown shoes.
Please colour Tom's clothes!

Who is who?

Miss Mouse, Mousey and Mike are good friends.

- Miss Mouse is not the smallest mouse.
- Mousey is not the first in line.
- Mike is smaller than Mousey.

Now, who is who?
Please write their names on the lines!

________________ ________________ ________________

Body-parts

Verbinde jedes Wort mit dem passenden Körperteil!

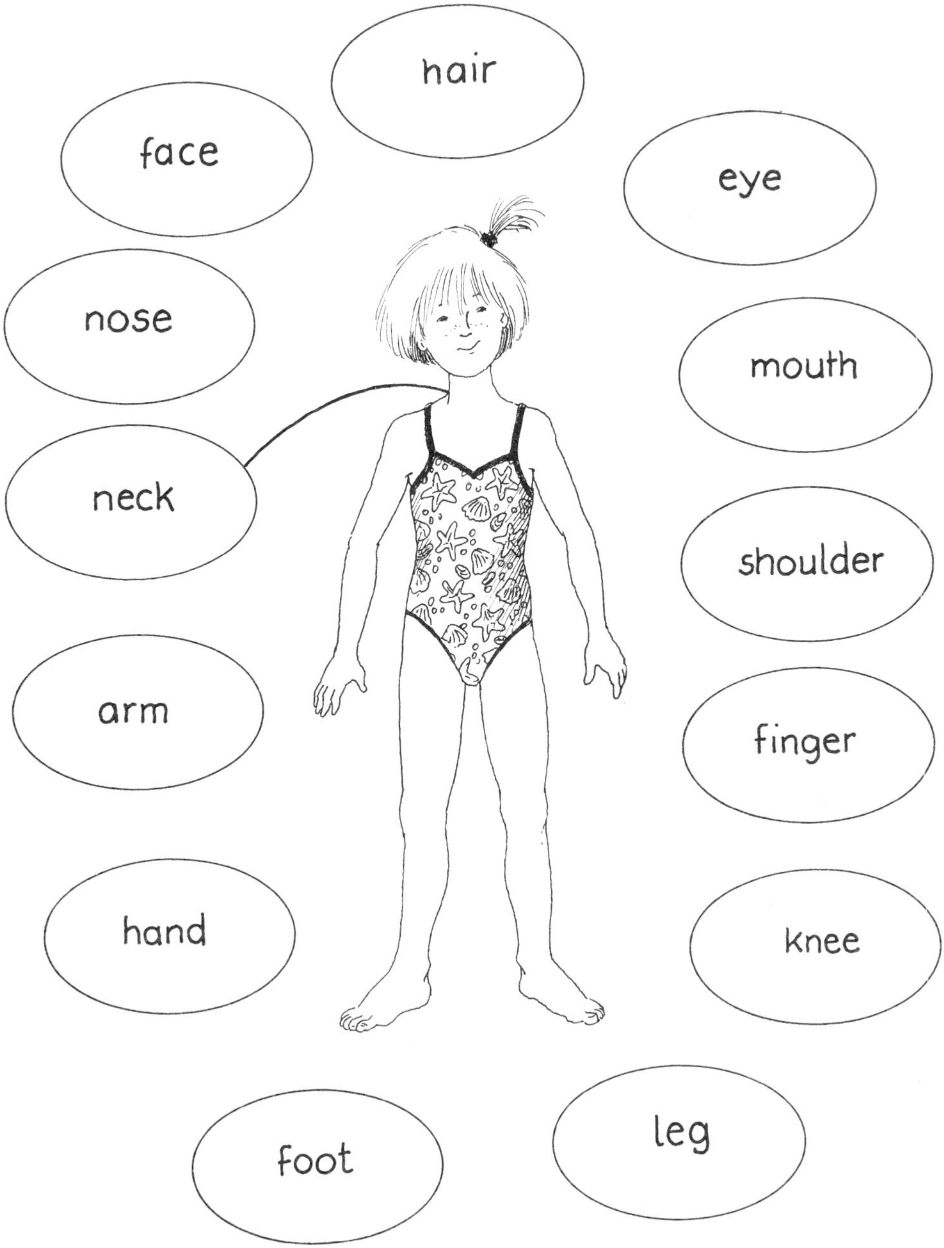

Family

Mike Grey
Betty Grey
Jo White
Lucy White
Diana Grey
Charles Grey
Bill Grey
Jane Grey
Kevin White
Baby Grey
Bob Grey
Mary Grey

- How is Mike Grey related to Bill Grey? He is his
- How is Kevin White related to Mary Grey? He is her
- How is Charles Grey related to Bill Grey? He is his
- How is Jane Grey related to Kevin White? She is his
- How is Betty Grey related to Charles Grey? She is his
- How is Diana Grey related to Bob Grey? She is his

Wenn du die dick umrandeten Buchstaben der Reihe nach hier einträgst, erhältst du den Namen von Baby Grey!

M

Numbers

Male jedes Kästchen mit einer der folgenden Zahlen aus, und du erhätst ein Bild.

thirty-five

eighty-eight

twenty-five

seventy-five

seventy-three

fifty-nine

seventy-eight

eighty-three

seventy-two

fifteen

fifty-eight

sixty-five

thirty-eight

ninety-four

sixteen

forty-five

fifty-five

seventy-four

seventy-seven

ninety-seven

seventy-six

ninety-five

seventy-nine

five

twenty-seven

fifty-seven

forty-nine

ninety-six

fifty-six

1	2	3	4	5	6	7	8	9	10
11	12	13	14	15	16	17	18	19	20
21	22	23	24	25	26	27	28	29	30
31	32	33	34	35	36	37	38	39	40
41	42	43	44	45	46	47	48	49	50
51	52	53	54	55	56	57	58	59	60
61	62	63	64	65	66	67	68	69	70
71	72	73	74	75	76	77	78	79	80
81	82	83	84	85	86	87	88	89	90
91	92	93	94	95	96	97	98	99	100

★ a car
★ a sailing-boat
★ a plane
★ a bicycle

Dinosaurs

Brontosaurus hat 15 Wörter verschluckt, die mit dem Buchstaben “c” beginnen. Kannst du sie entdecken?

Mit den Buchstaben auf Stegosaurus kannst du die Wörter unten vervollständigen.

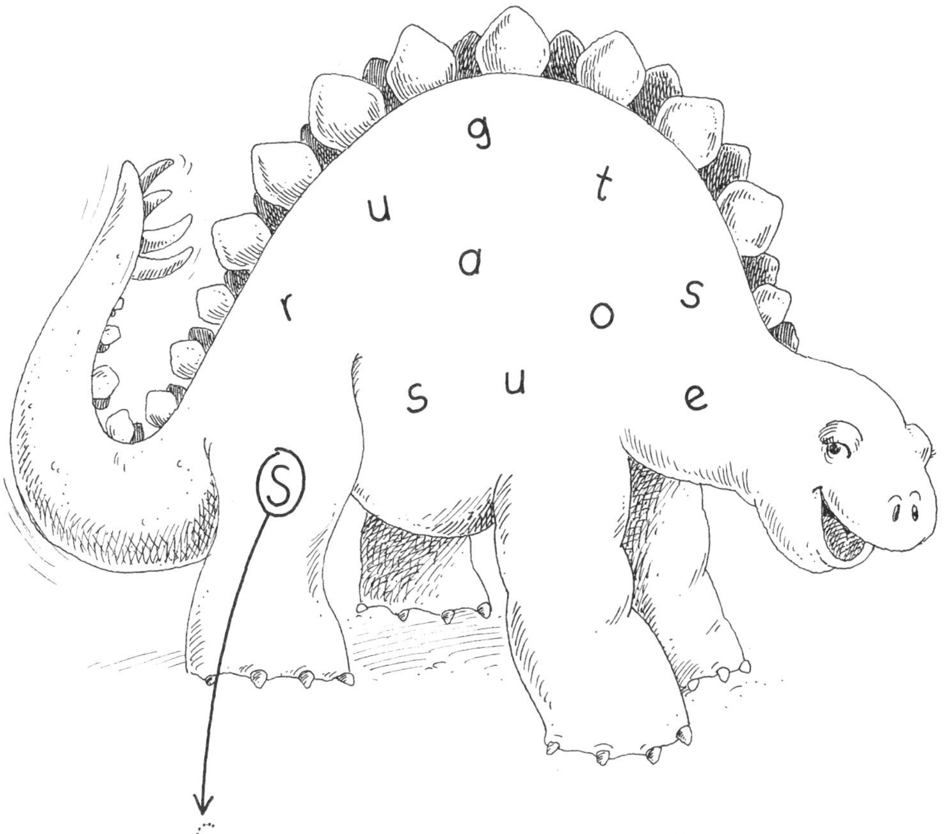

Sunday

r_ler

t_ee

mo_se

c_r

b_d

hor_e

_irl

b_y

_able

chee_e

What is Miss Mouse doing?

Suche die Verben im Buchstabengitter, kreise sie ein, und schreibe sie unter die passenden Bilder.

Achtung!
He, she, it, das “s” muß mit!
Schreibe also z. B.: she drinks

____

____

Wenn du alles richtig machst, bleiben im Gitter 7 Buchstaben übrig. Bilde daraus zwei weitere Verben, und schreibe sie hier neben die deutsche Bedeutung!

warten - ___________________

sehen - ___________________

___________________ ___________________ ___________________

she cries

she p s

she

l	i	s	t	e	n	w	w
a	i	c	l	e	a	n	r
s	l	e	e	p	e	d	i
r	p	l	a	y	a	r	t
e	c	r	y	t	t	e	e
a	d	r	i	v	e	a	r
d	s	f	e	e	d	m	u
t	h	i	n	k	e	e	n

Opposites

Kennst du das Gegenteil?

Trage die dick umrandeten Buchstaben der Reihe nach hier ein!

On the farm

Weißt du die Namen der abgebildeten Tiere und Gegenstände? Sie beginnen alle mit dem Buchstaben “h”.

1	h									
2	h									
3	h									
4	h									
5	h									
6	h									
7	h									
8	h									
9	h									
10	h									
11	h									
12	h									

12
8
7
9
6
5
4
10
1
11

Words with -oo

1

2

3

4

5

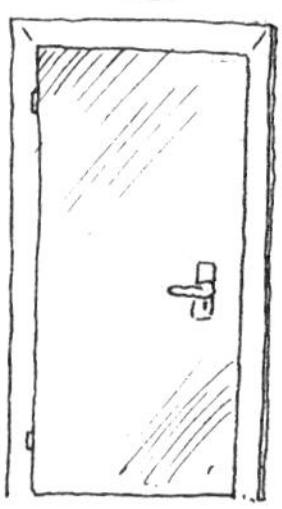

6

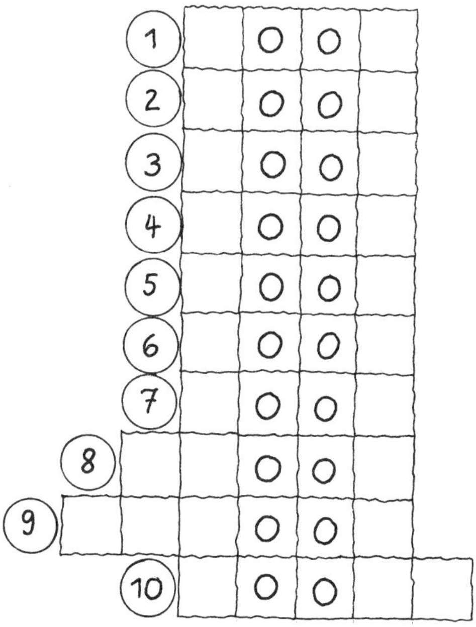

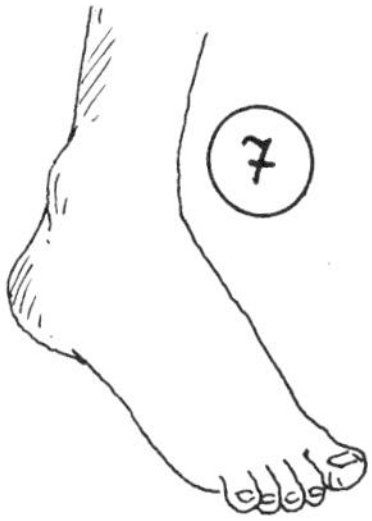

7

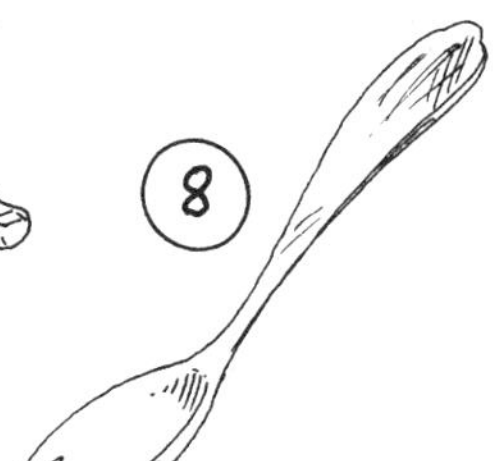

8

9

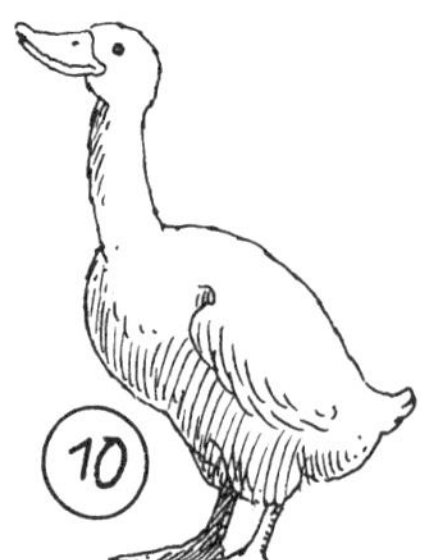

10

Words with -ee

1

2

3

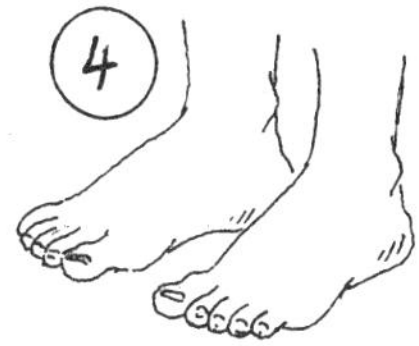

4

1				e	e		
2				e	e		
3				e	e		
4				e	e		
5				e	e		
6				e	e		
7				e	e		
8				e	e		
9				e	e		
10				e	e		

5

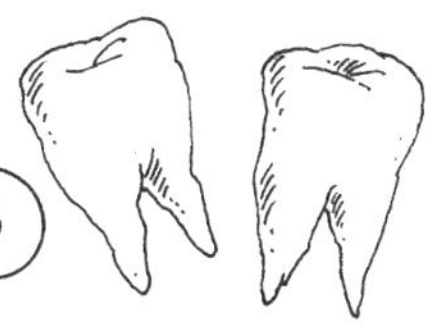

6

7

10

9

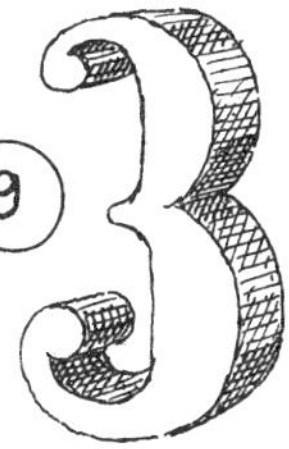

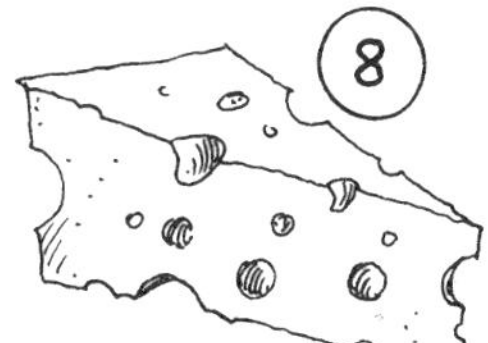

8

Horses

Der Bauer ist nicht da. Deshalb soll Sam heute die Pferde in ihre Boxen bringen. Aber welches Pferd kommt wohin? Kannst du helfen? Verbinde!

Wenn du alles richtig machst, sagen dir die Buchstaben auf den Pferden, was mit dem Bauer los ist.

Tom's room

cat	pencil	ball	goose	shoes	poster
radio	lamp	bed	chair	elephant	flag
scissors	satchel	table	trousers	toy-car	
blanket	apple	window	carpet	glass	
plate	T-shirts	train	straw	book	

Trage die Anfangsbuchstaben der 5 ausgestrichenen Wörter hier ein!

You are | | | | | | !

Butterflies

Wenn du die Wörter auf den Flügeln der Schmetterlinge ergänzt und die hinzugefügten Buchstaben zusammen liest, weißt du, wonach die Schmetterlinge suchen.

The butterflies are looking for ...

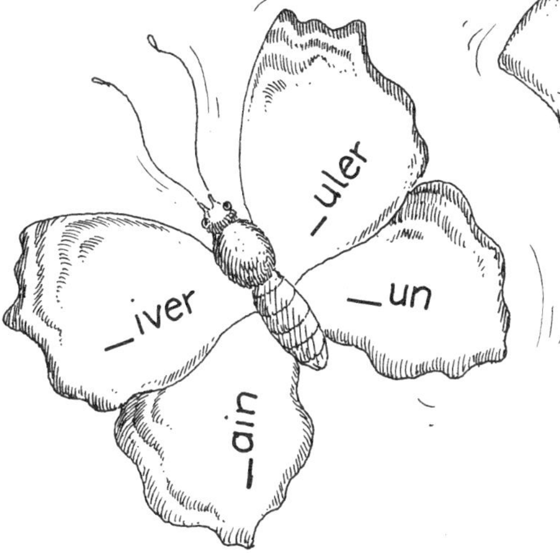

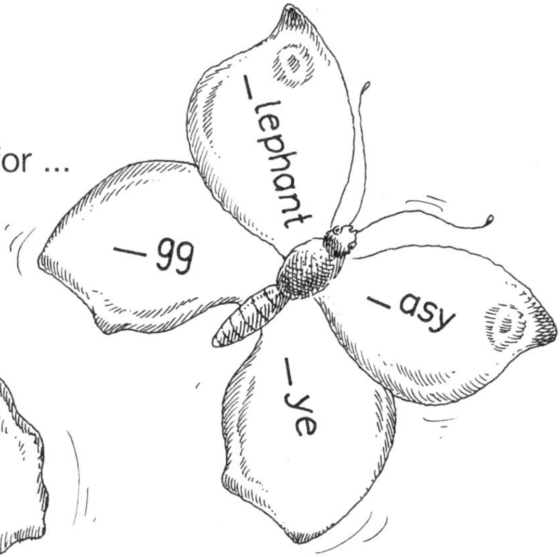

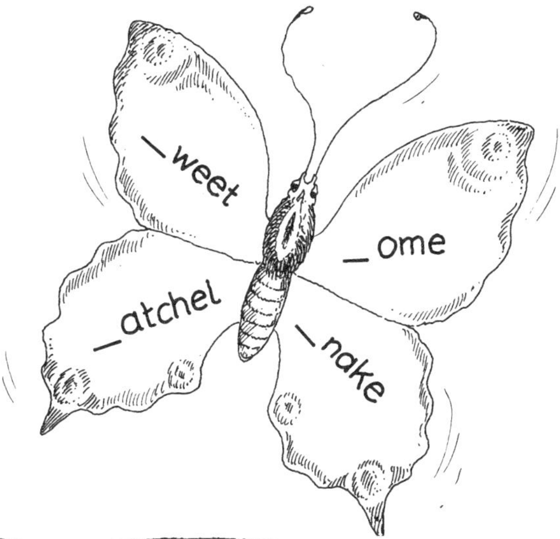

Tip: Alle 4 Wörter eines Schmetterlings beginnen mit demselben Buchstaben!

Let’s rhyme!

Male alle Blasen mit Wörtern, die sich reimen, in derselben Farbe aus!

hand
end
rat
me
grey
pay
sand
she
You'll need 5 different colours!

At the airport

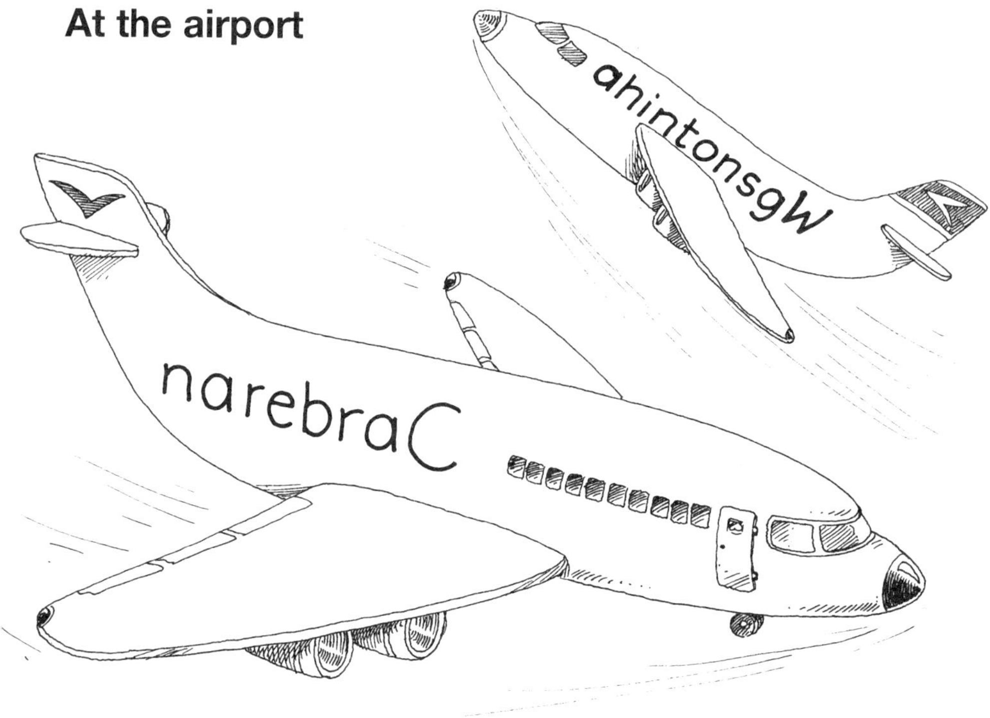

Die Flugzeuge fliegen zu großen englischen, amerikanischen oder australischen Städten. Ordne die Buchstaben, und kreise die 8 richtigen Städte ein!

Atlanta Canberra Washington Manchester Sydney

Bristol Aberdeen Denver London Chicago Adelaide

New York Perth Leeds Dallas Glasgow

Nouns and verbs

Schreibe das passende Verb unter das Bild!

verbs:

smell drive sleep draw write cut read drink
watch sit wear play cook ride

drive

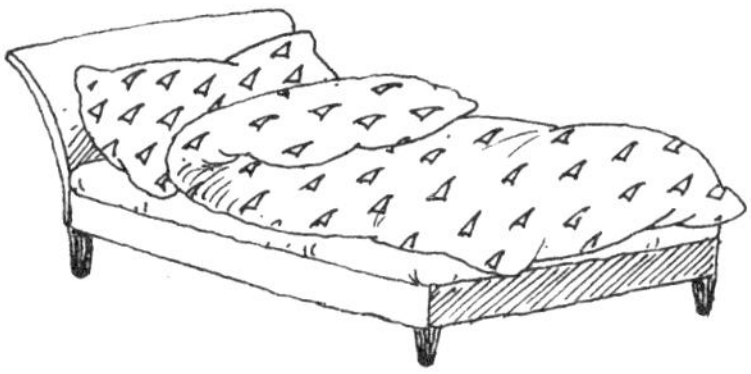

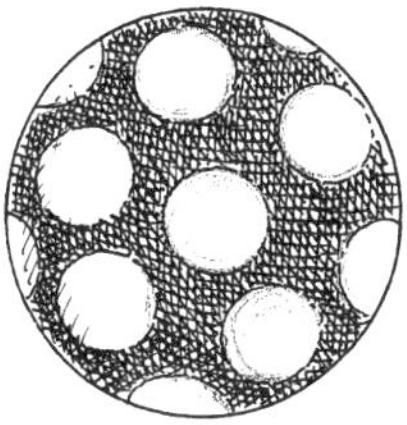

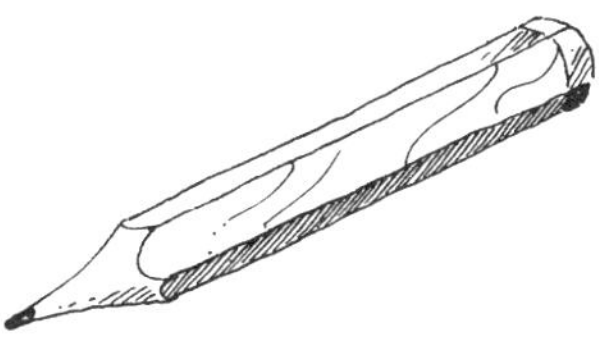

Miss Mouse is missing

Trage die entsprechenden Begriffe in das Rätselgitter ein, und du erfährst, wo sich Miss Mouse versteckt hat!

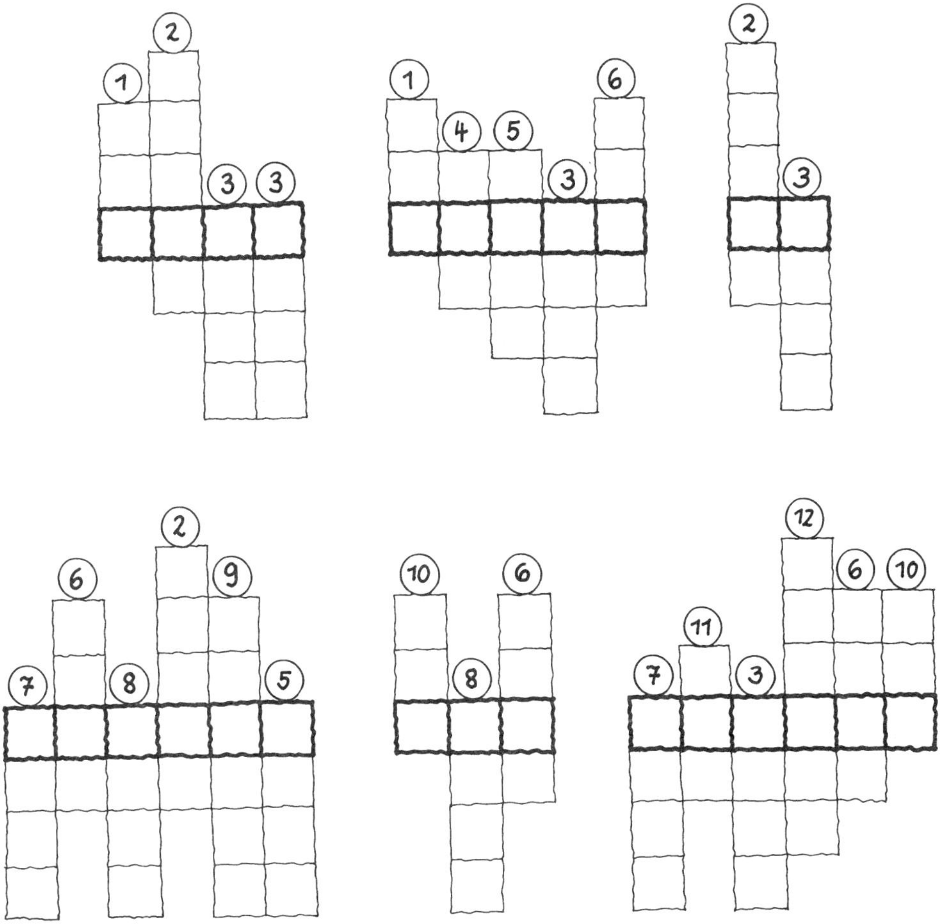

Rhyming pictures

Von 3 Bildern reimt sich jeweils eins nicht. Streiche es durch!

PARIS

At school

Dieses Rätsel hat zwei Teile. "Übersetze" zuerst die Zahlen in Buchstaben, und schreibe sie darunter, z. B.:

9	5	2	6	4	11
c	a	r	p	e	t

Verbinde dann jedes Wort mit dem passenden Bild!

2	3	8	8	4	2

6	4	7	9	12	1

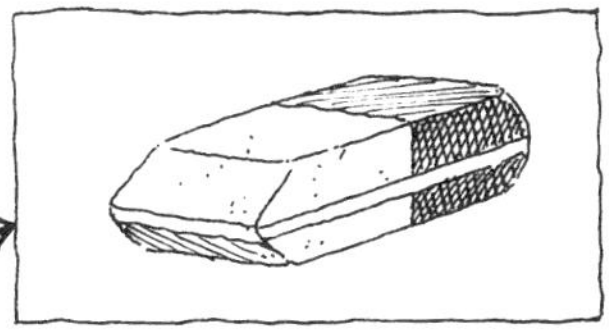

2	3	1	4	2

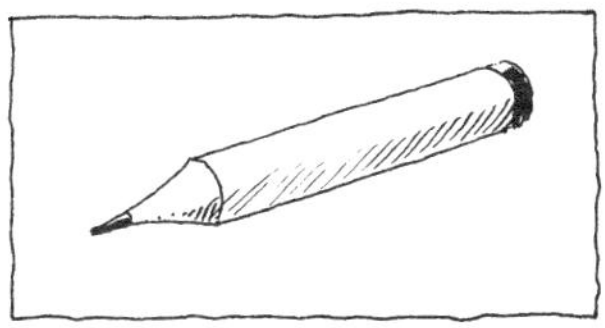

9	13	5	12	2

6	3	6	12	1

10	5	11	9	13	4	1

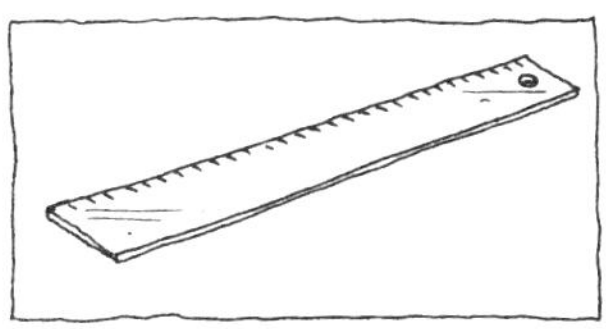

Jobs

Schreibe den jeweiligen Beruf unter das passende Bild! Die Silben im Kasten helfen dir dabei.

far- nur- ba- but- post- -mer

pi- tea- cap- -lot -cher

-man -se -ker -cher -tain

dentist

A lot to see in our town

Lies die Wörter auf der rechten Seite, und male diejenigen Felder mit Rotstift aus, in denen ein Begriff steht, den du im Bild sehen kannst.

flag	ball	star	table	man
sun	girl	zebra	tree	egg
lemon	frog	boy	moon	cup
knife	house	flower	car	spoon
woman	basket	ship	banana	street

Die ausgemalten Bilder ergeben zusammen einen Buchstaben. Welchen? Kreise ihn ein!

A X Z H S

New words

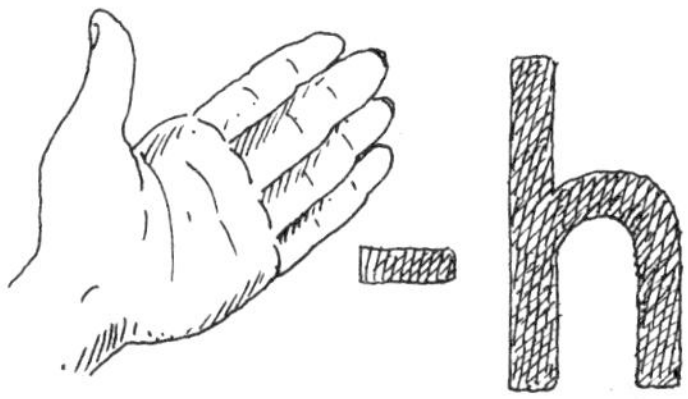

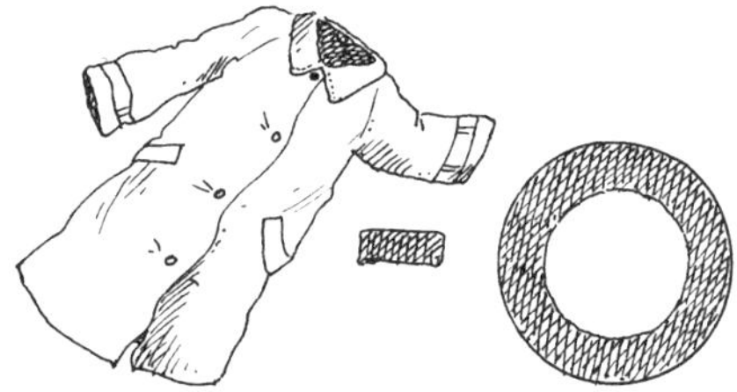

For example : hand - h = and

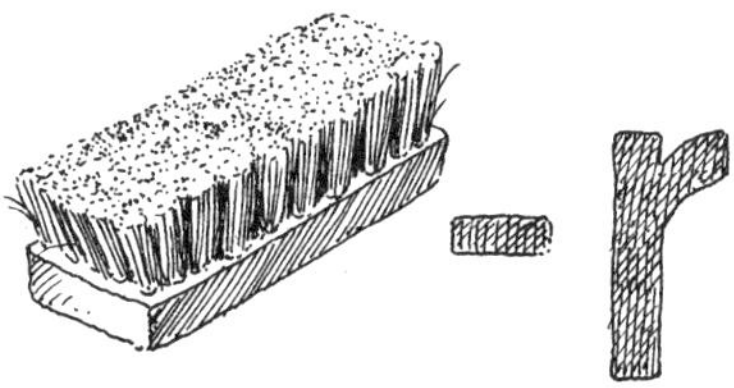

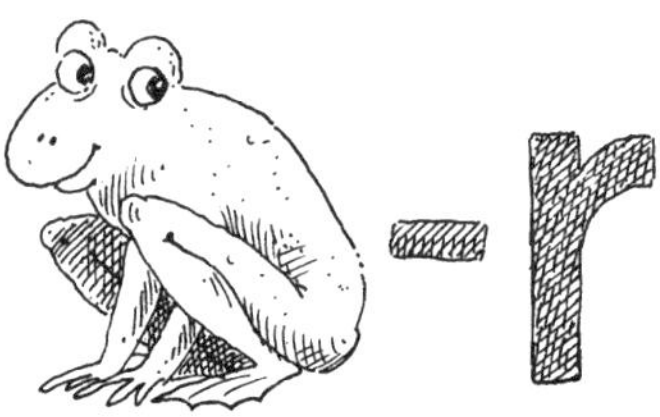

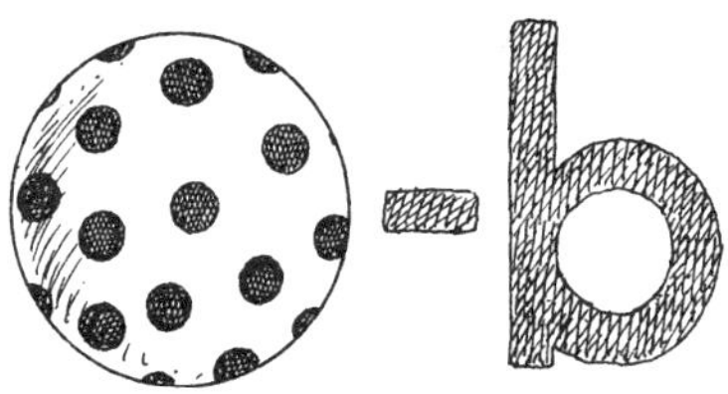

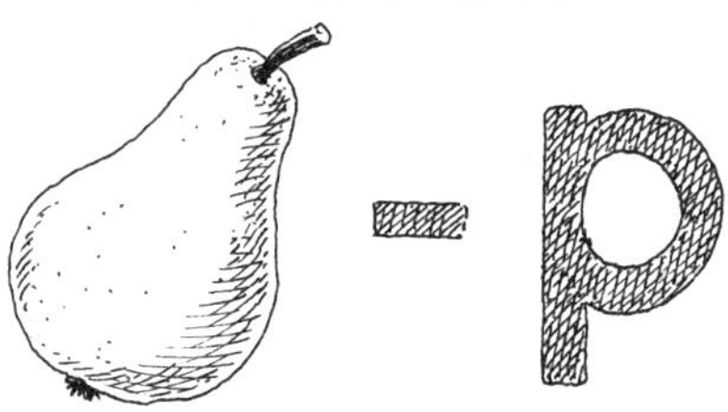

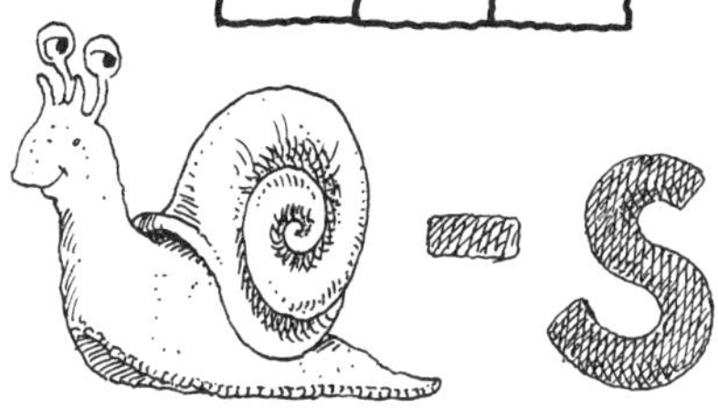

Numbers

Trage die ausgeschriebenen Zahlen in das Rätselgitter ein!

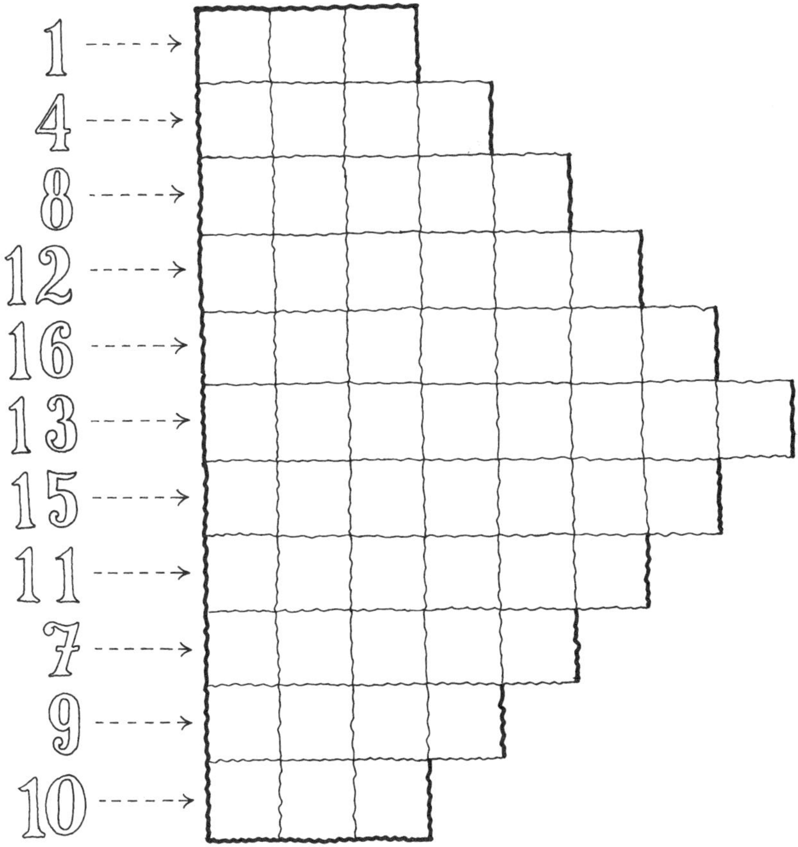

50	106
400	7863208

Pictures and sentences

Schreibe in das Kästchen hinter jedem Satz den Erkennungsbuchstaben des dazugehörigen Bildes!

The cat is on the chair.

Mrs. Brown is reading the newspaper.

Tom is cleaning the board.

The fish is in the basket.

The mouse is riding a bike.

The monkey is eating a banana.

Chris is reading a book.

Lucy goes shopping.

The children are laughing.

Bob is drawing a fish.

Picture Crossword

Trage den Namen jedes abgebildeten Gegenstands in das Kreuzworträtsel ein!

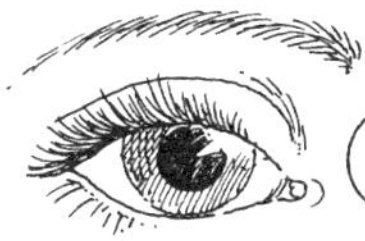

13

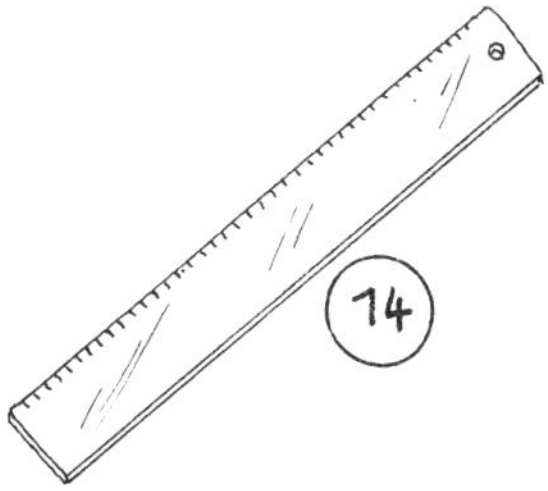

14

15

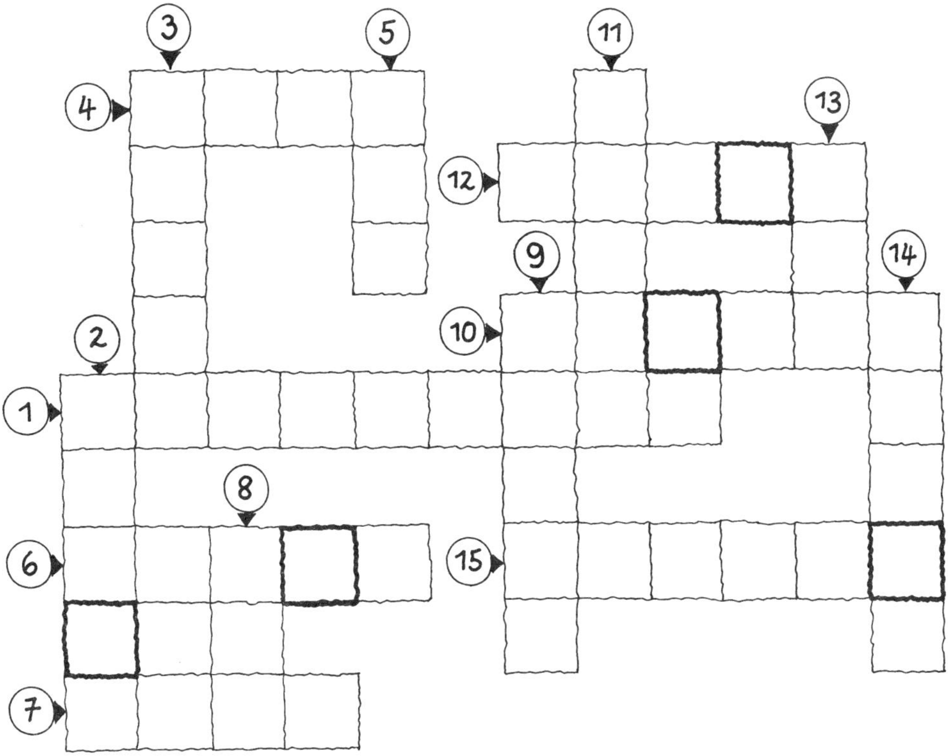

Wenn du die dick umrandeten Buchstaben hier einträgst, erhältst du das Lösungsmotto.

Aufgepaßt: Die richtige Reihenfolge der Buchstaben mußt du noch finden.

_ _ _ _ _ !

Colours

Welche Farben haben die abgebildeten Dinge in Wirklichkeit?
Trage die Farben ins Rätselgitter ein!

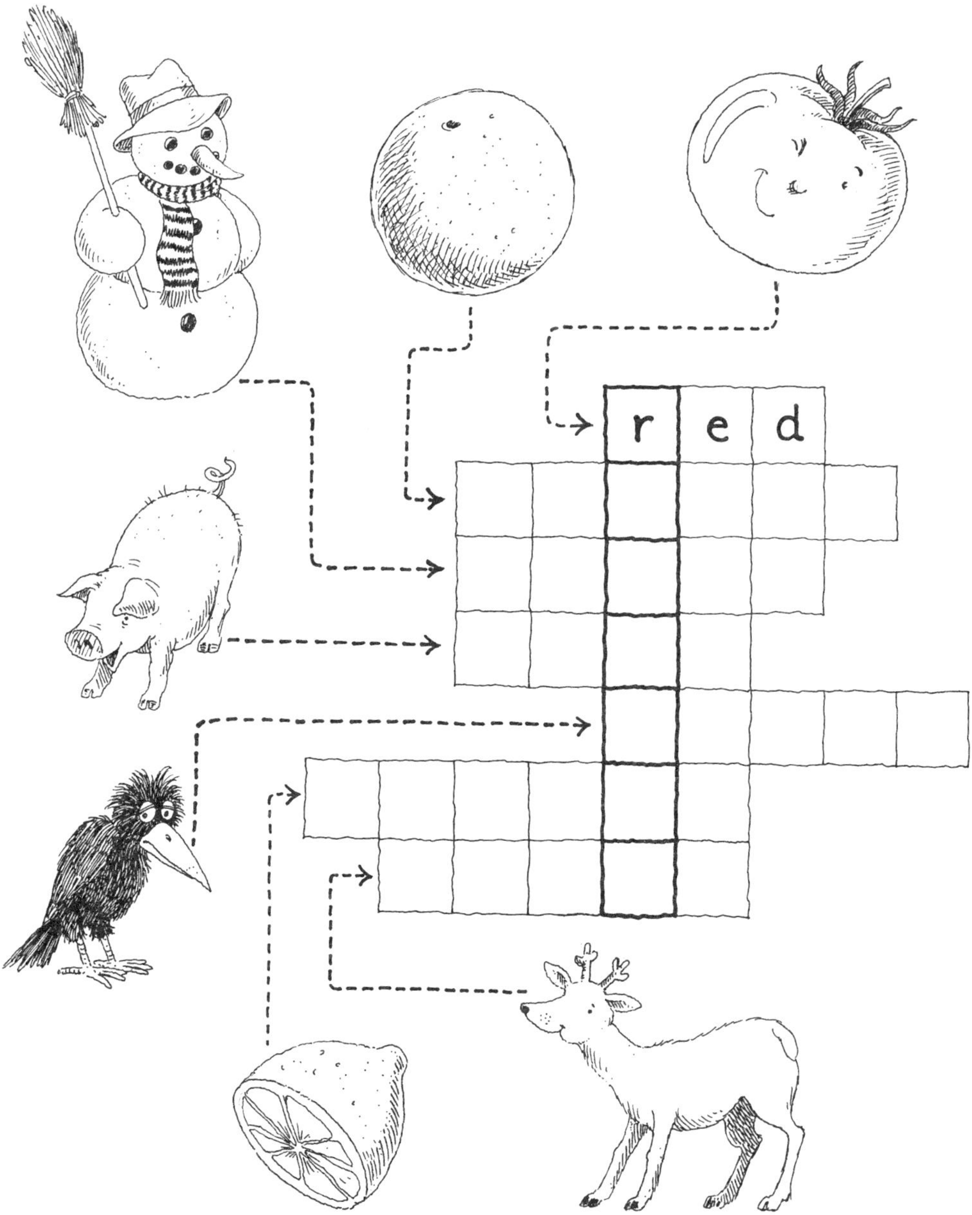

Male die Felder in den angegebenen Farben aus! Drehe das Bild um, wenn du fertig bist!

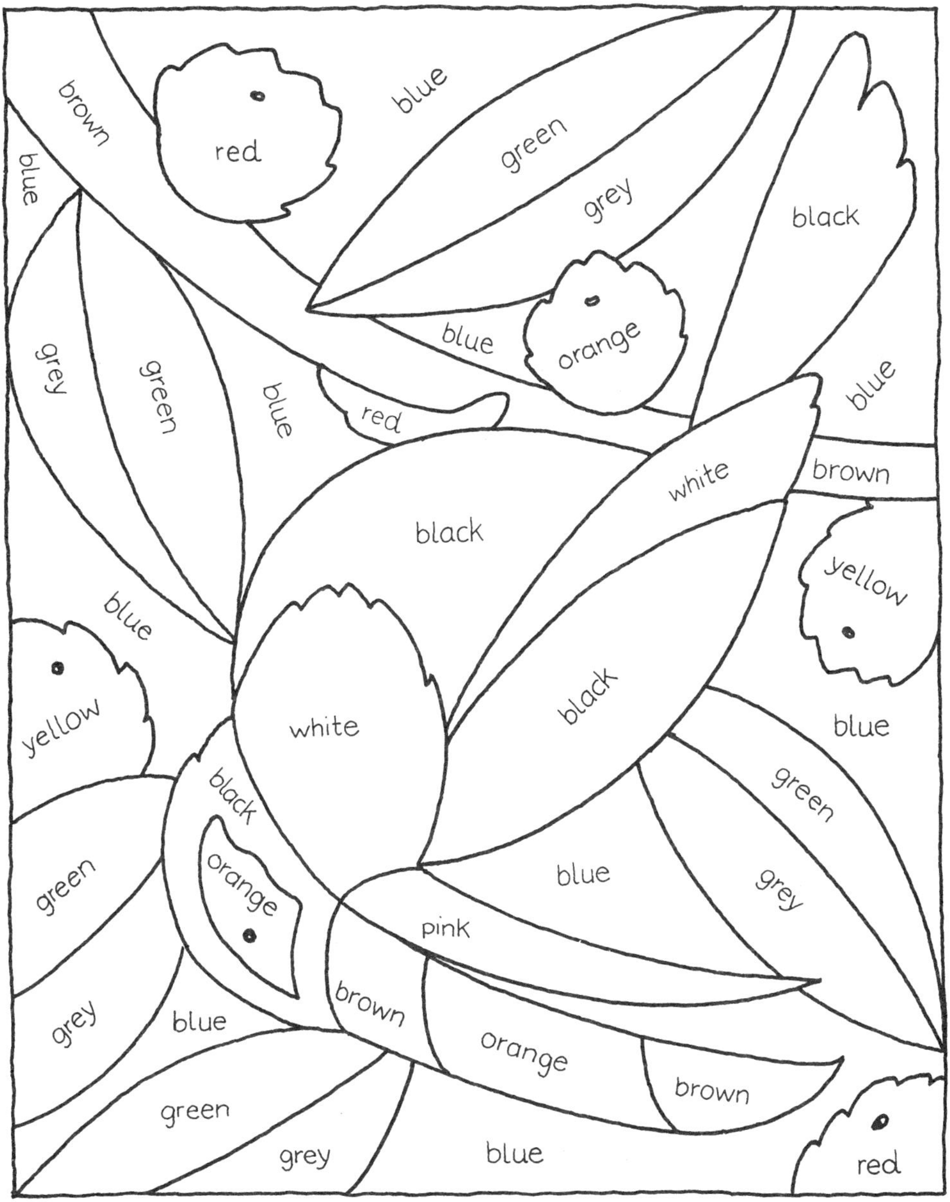

Complete the sentences!

Finde für jeden Satz die fehlende Präposition!

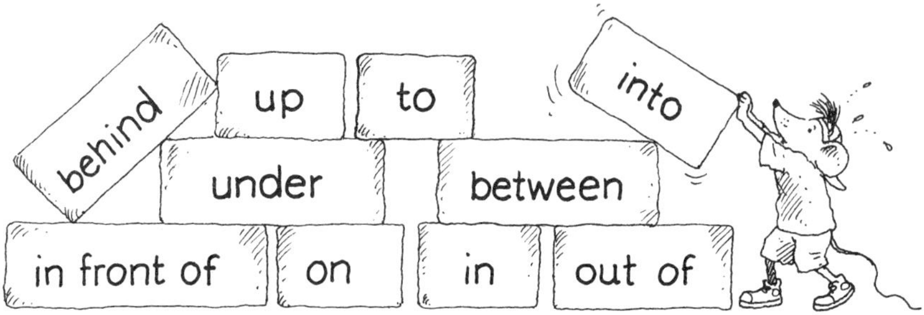

Miss Mouse is
going __________ school.

Miss Mouse
is sitting _______ a chair.

Miss Mouse
is ______________ a box.

Miss Mouse is
playing _______ the garden.

Miss Mouse is climbing
__________ a ladder.

Miss Mouse is going
_______ the house.

Miss Mouse is standing
_______ two cats.

Miss Mouse is reading
____________ the table.

Miss Mouse is looking
__________ the tent.

Miss Mouse
is __________ the shop.

Lösungen

Seite 2/3

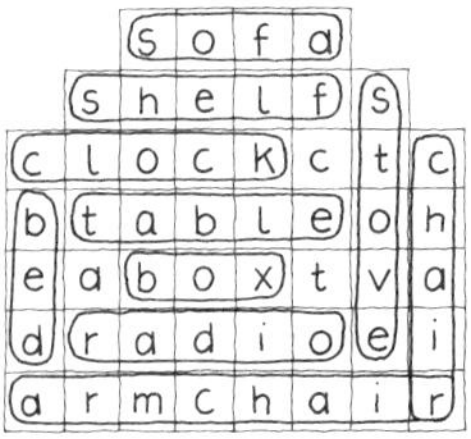

Lösung: It's a cat.

Seite 4/5

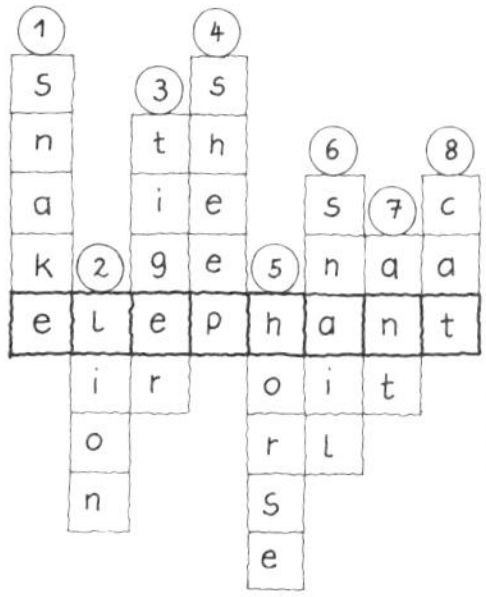

Seite 6/7

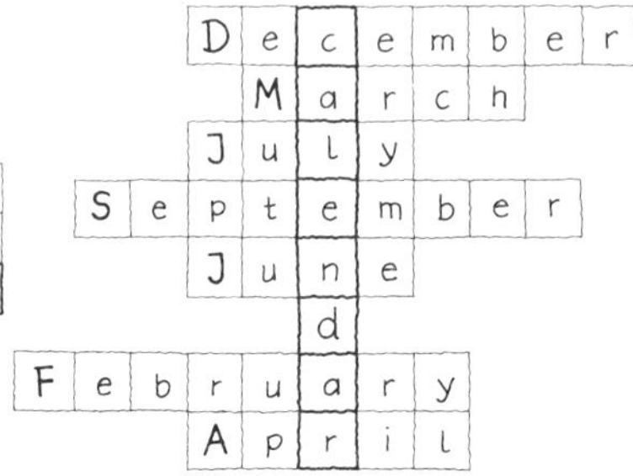

Seite 8/9

Anne is going to the cinema.
Mary is going to town.
Linda is going to the zoo.

Seite 10

sandwich, cake, bicycle

Seite 12

1st box: Miss Mouse
2nd box: Mousey
3rd box: Mike

Seite 13

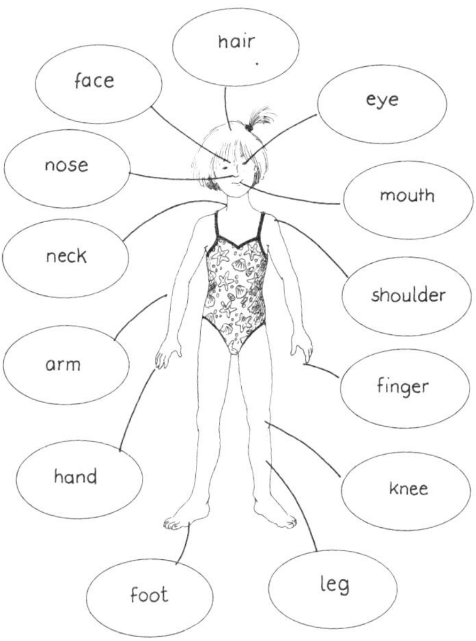

Seite 14/15

Mike Grey is Bill Grey's father.
Kevin White is Mary Grey's uncle.
Charles Grey is Bill Grey's brother.
Jane Grey is Kevin White's sister.
Betty Grey is Charles Grey's mother.
Diana grey is Bob Grey's aunt.
Baby Grey's name is Maureen.

Seite 16/17
a sailing-boat

Seite 18

Seite 19
Sunday, ruler, tree, mouse, car, bed, horse, girl, boy, table, cheese

Seite 20/21

l	i	s	t	e	n	w	w
a	i	c	l	e	a	n	r
s	l	e	e	p	e	d	i
r	p	l	a	y	a	r	t
e	c	r	y	t	t	e	e
a	d	r	i	v	e	a	r
d	s	f	e	e	d	m	u
t	h	i	n	k	e	e	n

she writes, cleans, reads, thinks, drives, cries, plays, sleeps, eats, listens, dreams, feeds, runs
warten - to wait
sehen - to see

Seite 22/23
fast - slow, sad - happy, right - left, last - first, near - far, over - under, open - closed, cold - hot, good - bad, false - true, light - heavy, off - on, long - short, winter - summer
Lösungssatz: You are a star!

Seite 24/25

1	h	e	n							
2	h	a	t							
3	h	u	t							
4	h	a	y							
5	h	a	n	d						
6	h	a	i	r						
7	h	o	r	n						
8	h	o	u	s	e					
9	h	o	r	s	e					
10	h	a	m	m	e	r				
11	h	a	m	s	t	e	r			
12	h	e	l	i	c	o	p	t	e	r

Seite 26

1			b	o	o	k	
2			r	o	o	m	
3			r	o	o	f	
4			m	o	o	n	
5			d	o	o	r	
6			c	o	o	k	
7			f	o	o	t	
8		s	p	o	o	n	
9	s	c	h	o	o	l	
10			g	o	o	s	e

Seite 27

1			b	e	e		
2			b	e	e	r	
3		t	r	e	e		
4			f	e	e	t	
5			g	e	e	s	e
6			t	e	e	t	h
7		s	h	e	e	p	
8		c	h	e	e	s	e
9	t	h	r	e	e		
10		q	u	e	e	n	

Seite 28/29
Lösungssatz: He is ill.

Seite 30/31
goose, radio, elephant, apple, train
Lösungssatz: You are great!

Seite 32/33
fruit, fish, field, fork
large, letter, lake, lemon
old, orange, open, out
window, wait, woman, watch
river, ruler, rain, run
elephant, easy, egg, eye
sweet, some, satchel, snake
Lösungssatz: The butterflies are looking for flowers.

Seite 34/35
cat, hat, fat, rat
tree, bee, me, she
land, hand, sand, end
ran, pan, hen, than
they, grey, pay, day

Seite 36/37
The aeroplanes go to:
Washington, Canberra, New York, Sydney, Manchester, London, Chicago, Leeds

Seite 38/39
car - drive, bed - sleep, picture - draw, nose - smell, clothes - wear, chair - sit, ball - play, TV - watch, pot - cook, tea - drink, knife - cut, book - read, horse - ride, pencil - write

Seite 40/41

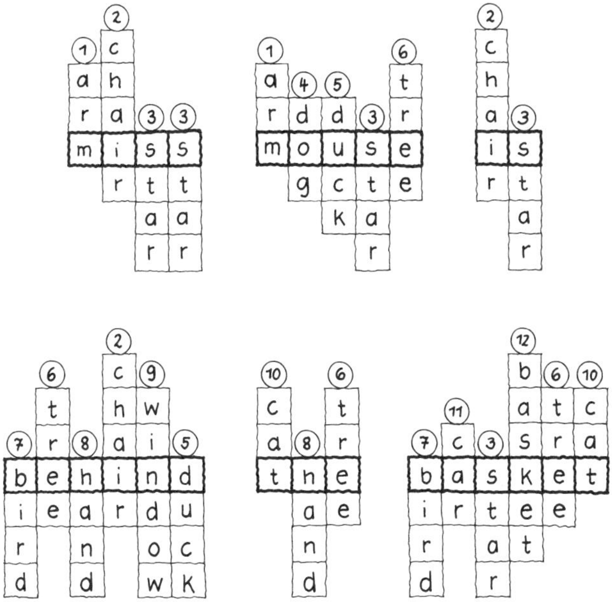

Seite 42/43

banana (box - fox), candle (boot - foot), apple (bee - tree), cake (moon - spoon), pott (boat - coat), bicycle (star - car), knife (hat - cat), telephone (pen - hen), ruler (cake - lake), house (frog - dog), book (shirt - skirt), cow (map - cap), pencil (house - mouse), car (clock - sock), bed (sun - gun), football (key - ski), flower (eight - plate), hand (rose - nose)

Seite 44/45

rubber, pencil, ruler, chair, pupil, satchel

Seite 46/47

dentist, farmer, butcher, pilot, teacher, postman, nurse, baker, captain

Seite 48/49

Im Bild: flag, man, girl, tree, boy, house, car, woman, street
Lösungsbuchstabe: x

Seite 50

coat - o = cat
feather - e = father
brush - r = bush
frog - r = fog
ball - b = all
pear - p = ear
snail - s = nail

Seite 51
one, four, eight, twelve, sixteen, thirteen, fifteen, eleven, seven, nine, ten
If you add all the numbers, you get 106.

Seite 52/53
Lösungswörter: super, great

Seite 57
This bird is a tucan.

Seite 58/59
Miss Mouse is going to school.
Miss Mouse is sitting on a chair.
Miss Mouse is behind a box.
Miss Mouse is playing in the garden.
Miss Mouse is climbing up a ladder.
Miss Mouse is going into the house.
Miss Mouse is standing between two cats.
Miss Mouse is reading under the table.
Miss Mouse is looking out of the tent.
Miss Mouse is in front of the shop

Seite 54/55

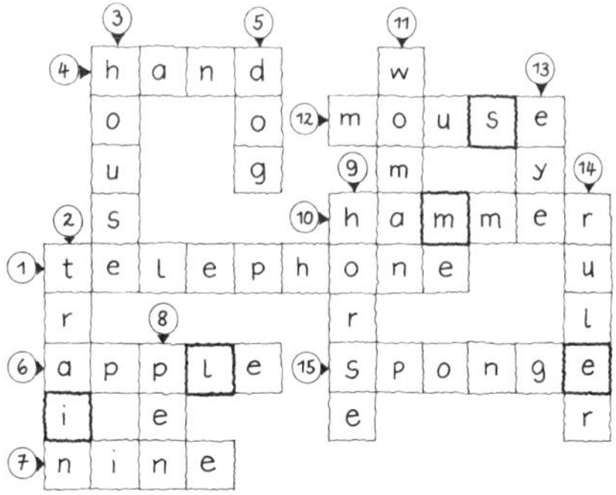

Seite 56

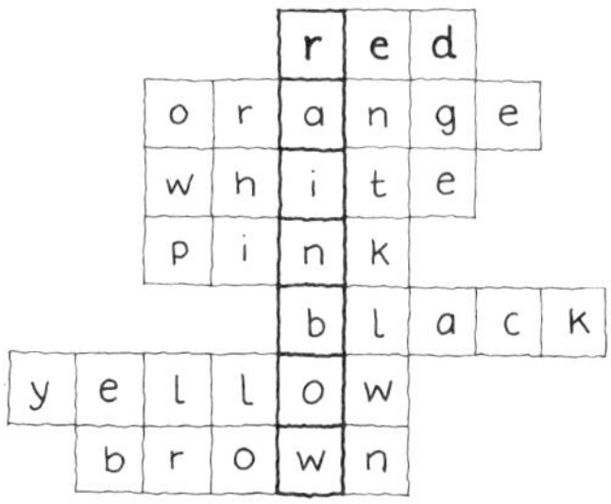

Lösungswort: rainbow

Die Deutsche Bibliothek - CIP-Einheitsaufnahme
Rätseln mit Spaß Englisch / Almuth Bartl.
Ill. von Angela Weinhold. - München : Ars-Ed., 1996
ISBN 3-7607-4655-1

99 98 97 5 4 3 2

Ausstattung und Herstellung: arsEdition, München
Umschlaggestaltung: Angela Weinhold
Printed in Italy

ISBN 3-7607-4655-1